REX Collections

JEFF BENCH

A classic early shot of the band by Ray Stevenson, attempting one of the best-known feats in the *Guinness Book of Records*. This became the basis for an early Pistols flyer.

Reynolds & Hearn Ltd
London

First published in 2005 by
Reynolds & Hearn Ltd
61a Priory Road
Kew Gardens
Richmond
Surrey TW9 3DH

Images © Rex Features 2005
Text © Reynolds & Hearn 2005

A CIP catalogue for this book is available from the British Library.

ISBN 1-90528-705-4

Designed by James King.

Printed and bound in Great Britain by
Biddles Ltd, King's Lynn, Norfolk.

NEVER MIND THE CONTENTS...

GB 76

'This crisis cannot possibly be resolved within parliament alone' David Stirling, former SAS leader and co-founder of GB75, a para-military organization formed to prevent anarchy breaking out in the UK

The 'National Happiness Index', a measure of social and economic progress (devised, in their wisdom, by the New Economics Foundation), has designated 1976 as the year in which the United Kingdon achieved its highest-ever recorded level of national wellbeing. The UK is now more wealthy and more technologically advanced, but its overall quality of life has apparently declined.

It's a difficult conclusion to stomach for anyone who remembers actually being alive in Britian in the mid-1970s. Happy times? The Bay City Rollers. The last season of *The Black and White Minstrel Show.* The last gasp of flares. Tension in the inner cities.'Troubles' in Northern Ireland. The long hot summer of drought. Images of parched reservoirs. The economy stagnating. Inflation stuck at 20 per cent. Unemployment beginning to rise. The International Monetary Fund bailing out the British Economy. Disappointment for the British team at the Montreal Olympics. And - a final indignity - even South-African born England cricket captain Tony Grieg grovelling in public to the West Indies team, after his rash boasts of 'making them grovel' had backfired. The traditional British establishment was firmly on the back foot.

Ezra Pound (like David Stirling, politically on the extreme right) once remarked that 'artists are the antennae of the race'. In this case, the artists seemed to have more of clue than the economists to what was really happening in Britian in 1976. The antennae of those drawn into the punk movement sensed something rotten in the world of stack heels and stagflation. Clichés abound as to what this really was. It has been labelled as a disillusionment stemming from the hyper-optimism of the previous decade. It has been described as a natural extension of the glam rock culture of the early seventies. Historians find social and economic explanations. Sociologists talk about sub-cultures. The religious right point to a decline in family values and the influence of television. Hip journalists adduce everything from MC5 to the Situationists to *Starsky and Hutch.* Richard Hell (of Richard Hell and the Voidoids) says he thought the whole thing up in New York, long before anyone in England had any idea...

Many have tried to take the credit (or blame) for punk. But facts are facts. On 6 November 1975, a band called the Sex Pistols had played their first gig at Saint Martin's School of Art in Central London. The band members called themselves Paul Cook, Steve Jones, Glen Matlock and Johnny Rotten. Their manager was a man called Malcolm McLaren...

Paul Cook, Steve Jones, Glen Matlock and Johnny Rott[en] cavort in Trafalgar Square.

Majestic Studios, 15 May 1976, left to right:
Jones, Lydon, Matlock, Cook, Malcolm
McLaren and Nils Stevenson

I WAS A
TEENAGE SE

'The human louse somewhat resembles
a tiny lobster, and he lives chiefly in your
trousers.' George Orwell, Homage to Catalonia

The earliest origins of the Sex Pistols go back to 1972, when school buddies Paul Cook, Steve Jones and Wally Nightingale formed a band called The Strand (named after the Roxy Music hit). The following year, the band members began to hang out at Malcolm McLaren's chelsea boutique Let It Rock. Del Noones, another frequent visitor to the shop, was added to the band on bass. The band's name was also changed to The Swankers (already a taste for off-colour puns was manifesting itself). In 1974 Noones was replaced by Stephen Hayes, who was later replaced by Let It Rock sales clerk Glen Matlock.

In1975 McLaren's store famously changed its name to Sex, and McLaren started to take a serious interest in the peculiar band which seemed to revolve around the store. McLaren began to mould the band into a more extreme version of itself. In August of 1975 John Lydon was persuaded to audition by miming to an Alice Cooper track, 'Eighteen'. Lydon himself says that Clash manager Bernie Rhodes persuaded him to pick up the microphone and have a go. More significantly, Lydon (now re-named Johnny Rotten on account of his grungy teeth), had already arrived at a style and attitude in mannerisms and dress that was a 'street' equivalent to McLaren's Situationist-inlfuenced ideas on band image

and promotion. McLaren saw the potential in Lydon and Lydon, underneath his cynical pose, was rather pleased to be asked to join a band.

'Malcolm asked me if I wanted to be in a band. I thought they must be joking.' John Lydon

Lydon was in and Nightingale was out. The legend has it that Nightingale was sacked for being 'too musically proficient', though another version of this story is that Nightingale was just 'too nice' for a band that was now planning to base its appeal on the confrontational posture that would evolve into punk. Nightingale also didn't really look the part in the way the other band members did. Bespectacled and scholarly-looking, he did not have the physical presence of Cook, Jones or Matlock. The Swankers was also now not considered an appropriate name for a band coming under McLaren's influence and featuring Lydon's harsh, sneering vocal style. Various other suggested names were thrown out, including The Damned, which was co-incidentally adopted as the name for Dave Vanian's later band. The name the Sex Pistols suited the band perfectly, but it is a matter of claim and counter-claim as to who actually thought it up.

'None of the others would have formed a group. Paul was heavily into an apprenticeship as an electrician. Steve was going to be a petty criminal, as simple as that. Stephen Hayes just ended up being a punk, a weak personality. I was the only one who could play.' Wally Nightingale

The newly-named Sex Pistols' career got off to a rocky start when the three other band members declined to turn up to the first rehearsal in early September. They didn't take to Rotten and didn't believe that McLaren was serious about the new line-up. But by late September, the band were hard at work, rehearsing daily at the studios above the Rose and Crown in Wandsworth, with McLaren picking up the tab. Their first gig would be at Saint Martins College of Art, on 6 November. Over the coming months, the Pistols slogged around the country, playing gigs to small crowds for little money, supporting other bands, and experiencing a lot of negative reactions. But, in the process, they found that they were also building a loyal and wildly enthusiastic following. Most loyal of these were the South London 'Bromley Contingent', whose members included Siouxsie Sioux, Steve Severin and Sid Vicious.

Chelsea School of Art, 5 December 1975. Left to right: John Stevens (probably), Sid Vicious, Paul Cook, Catwoman.

An early gig at El Paradise Club, Soho, 4 April 1976, John still in the DIY ripped-sweater look.

In full flight, El Paradise Club, 4 April 1976.

John's home-made 'I Hate Pink Floyd' tee shirt was a successful early statement of his position on prog rock.

John takes a break, 100 Club, 31 August 1976.

THE PROBLE IS YOU!

...she was not a true prostitute for she was the object on which men prostituted themselves

Angela Carter, from 'The Loves of Lady Purple'

The Sex Pistols pose in Berwick Street, Soho, April 1976, in front of some adverts for softcore sex films. These were the days before home video, when men dressed in the legendary 'dirty macs' were forced to leave their homes in order watch x-rated films in the proverbial 'clean, well-lit places'.

STEVE

JONES

Steve Jones was born on 3 September 1955, in
London. He grew up in Shepherds Bush, a non-descript
and somewhat down-at-heel neighbourhood, but
also an important crossroads for many activities and
communities in West London. Jones started playing
guitar in the early seventies, and was influenced by the
then-current glam rock movement, including T Rex, as
well as The Faces, the Stooges and Johnny Thunders
of the New York Dolls. Jones, being poor, was forced
to acquire a lot of his equipment illicitly from other
artistes, including allegedly pinching a guitar from David
Bowie's sidesman Mick Ronson. Jones later explained
that the missing grille on his Les Paul had been taken
off to remove the name of the previous owner. Despite
his superficial couldn't-care-less-attitude to technique,
Jones is a highly talented guitarist and was at every
stage the mainspring behind the Sex Pistols' music,
live and in the studio. Since the break-up of the Pistols,
Jones has been in regular demand as a guitarist by acts
as various as Thin Lizzy and Iggy Pop.

GLEN MATLOCK

Glen Matlock was born on 27 August 1957. A music fan from the age of six, his childhood favourites were the Beatles ('Twist and Shout') and The Kinks ('You Really Got Me'). After leaving secondary school he attended Saint Martins College of Art, and also absorbed similar glam rock influences to Steve Jones. In 1974, working as an assistant in Malcolm McLaren's shop, he got to know McLaren, Cook and Jones, and became the Sex Pistols' bass player. McLaren regarded Matlock as 'an anchor of normality' in the group. Even after Matlock formally left the Sex Pistols in February 1977, he still continued to be involved with the band. According to Lydon, Matlock played bass on *Never Mind The Bollocks*, as well as coaching replacement Sid Vicious to improve the latter's rudimentary skills as a bass player. After leaving the Pistols, Matlock formed The Rich Kids, along with Rusty Egan, Steve New and Midge Ure. Matlock also backed Sid Vicious during Sid's solo live shows in 1978.

Glen Matlock's book *I Was A Teenage Sex Pistol* was published in 1990.

PAUL COOK

Paul Cook was born on 20 July 1956, in West London. Cook first
played drums as a teenager. After leaving school, he became
an apprentice electrician, but also remained friends with Steve
Jones and Wally Nightingale, who together made up the core
of The Swankers. Cook's powerful drumming is at the core of
the Sex Pistols' sound. Busy, explosive, full of sudden kicks and
unexpected fills, it's the ingredient that gives the music that 'always
about to boil over' sensation. After the break-up of the Sex Pistols,
Cook formed The Professionals with Steve Jones, and was later
part of eighties rock contenders The Chiefs of Relief.

JOHN LyDON

John Lydon was born on 31 January 1956, in Finsbury Park, North London. His mother and father were Irish, and the family was poor and working class. At seven he suffered from severe spinal meningitis, and experienced comas and memory loss. Lydon's intense stare is said to have had its origin in this childhood illness.

A talented misfit at school, Lydon was expelled from his Catholic Secondary School but completed his education successfully at Hackney & Stoke Newington College of Further Education and at Kingsway College. He began to develop his anti-fashion style of dress: his interest in outré clothing led to his visits to Sex in the King's Road, and to his surprise audition for the Sex Pistols. Transforming from Lydon to Rotten, John became the creative force behind the Pistols' lyrics, and carefully masked his intelligence and poetic turn of phrase behind a superficially mindless posture. Lydon's taste in music as varied as Miles Davis, Neil Young, Can and Captain Beefheart has informed his post-Sex Pistols career with Public Image Ltd. His uncompromising honesty and ability to puncture pomposity and hypocrisy continue to fuel his writing and broadcasting career.

The 100 Club gig on 30 March 1976

Classic publicity shots for Seditionaries,
featuring Vivienne Westwood herself,
Jordan and Chrissie Hynde.

ONE INNOCENT

'This Freak was divided completely in half - the left side was a man and the right side a woman. The costume on the left was a leopard skin and on the right side a brassiere and a spangled skirt' Carson McCullers, *The Member of the Wedding*

At the moment of economic abundance, the concentrated result of social labor becomes visible and subjugates all reality to appearance, which is now its product. Capital is no longer the invisible centre which directs the mode of production: its accumulation spreads it all the way to the periphery in the form of tangible objects. The entire expanse of society is its portrait. Guy Debord, *Society of the Spectacle*

COMPULSORY BACKGROUND SECTION
ON THE TRUE MEANING OF PUNK

A sociologist explains:

Blah blah subculture blah blah resistance through rituals blah blah faceless housing estates blah blah youth unemployment blah blah inner city boredom blah blah Britain's declining position in the world blah blah litter-strewn backstreets blah blah the miners' strikes of 1972 and 1974 blah blah class conflict blah blah Paris 1968 blah blah collapse of traditional working-class communities blah blah media hegemony blah blah mods skinheads suedeheads rude boys blah blah Frank Bough

A music journalist interjects:

Blah blah MC5 *Kick Out The Jams* blah blah Iggy Pop and the Stooges blah blah The Pretty Things blah blah Glam Rock blah blah New York art punk scene blah blah Television blah blah Tom Verlaine blah blah New York Dolls blah blah Ramones blah blah UK Pub Rock blah blah Eddie and the Hot Rods blah blah Dr Feelgood blah blah Junior Murvin and reggae influence on The Clash blah blah massive pomp rock stadium concerts blah blah Emerson Lake & Palmer, Jethro Tull, Pink Floyd, Yes blah blah street credibility blah blah relevance blah blah small record labels blah blah reinvention of the single blah blah pogoing blah blah all over really by the end of 1976

A costume historian continues the story:

Blah blah fashion as social confrontation blah blah safety pins blah blah tartan blah blah ironic swastikas blah blah bondage blah blah deep cultural origins of ripped clothing in the Landsknecht movement of the fifteenth century blah blah corsets and the female body as contested locus of political signification blah blah challenging the male gaze blah blah Nina Hagen

A style guru clarifies a few more points of importance:

Blah blah King's Road blah blah Sex blah blah Seditionaries blah blah Jamie Reid blah blah Suburban Press blah blah Vivienne Westwood blah blah Jordan blah blah Chrissie Hynde blah blah Bromley Contingent blah blah Sue Catwoman blah blah Siouxsie Sioux blah blah Adam Ant blah blah fabulous parties at Andrew Logan's place blah blah most important movement of the twentieth century

Adam Ant with Jordan

Left: Pauline Murray of Penetration.
Right: Brian James of The Damned.

Malcolm McLaren and Vivienne Westwood.

The Damned: Brian James and Captain Sensible.

Right: Jordan

ATCHA GONNA DO ABOUT IT?

'Have you ever noticed that there's always too much weather in England? ... It rains, or it doesn't rain. They're never happy.' John Lydon, from Rotten: No Irish, No Blacks, No Dogs

Contact sheets from a Ray Stevenson photo session that yielded one of the most often reproduced images of John.

'He knew damn well he was making me uncomfortable'

John D MacDonald, *The Executioners*

In Britain's so-called temperate climate, exceptionally hot summers come along about once a decade. 1947: all still on the ration books, but open again for business after World War Two. 1959: Buddy Holly and The Day The Music Died. 1966: the Beatles, *Revolver* and 'Good Day Sunshine'. 1976: the mother of all droughts, drain smells in South London and an ominous sense of disquiet that was perfectly embodied by the punk movement. Pictures of dessicated reservoirs, when published, were regarded as portraits of the parched national psyche. And then, in the Autumn of 1976, record rainfall. A new climate of extremes seemed to prevail.

On 20-21 September the 100 Club in London's Oxford Street held its first 'Punk Festival'. The Sex Pistols had been playing a regular Tuesday night residency there earlier in the year. The 100 Club was (and still is) a venue more associated with jazz and blues of all kinds, as a study of the names of forthcoming attractions captured in the photographs of the 100 Club gigs will illustrate. The Sex Pistols topped the bill on 20 September: Subway Sect, Siouxsie and the Banshees, the Clash and the Stinky Toys also played. The following night, when The Damned, The Vibrators and The Buzzcocks played (but not the Sex Pistols), there was trouble when Number One fan Sid Vicious reputedly threw a glass at the stage, flying splinters causing injuries. Despite having no direct connection with the incident, the Pistols were banned from the 100 Club. By this time the Sex Pistols were also banned from playing at various other London venues, including Dingwalls, the Marquee, and the Rock Garden. Nevertheless, the energy generated by the 100 Club gigs fired up the British music press, with both *Melody Maker* and *Sounds* reporting the gigs and running major editorial features on the Punk Rock phenomenon. Suddenly, whatever the Pistols did or didn't do was news, at least within the music press. Under McLaren's management, the band signed a recording contract with EMI in September, and began work on their first single.

Screen on the Green, 29 August 1976.
Left: Malcolm McLaren and Paul Cook, Wessex Studio, 17 October 1976.
The Chris Thomas recording session for 'Anarchy In The UK'.

Paul and Steve in a rare outdoor shot.

DIY Punk, 1976. The Rotten
look before the designer makeover.

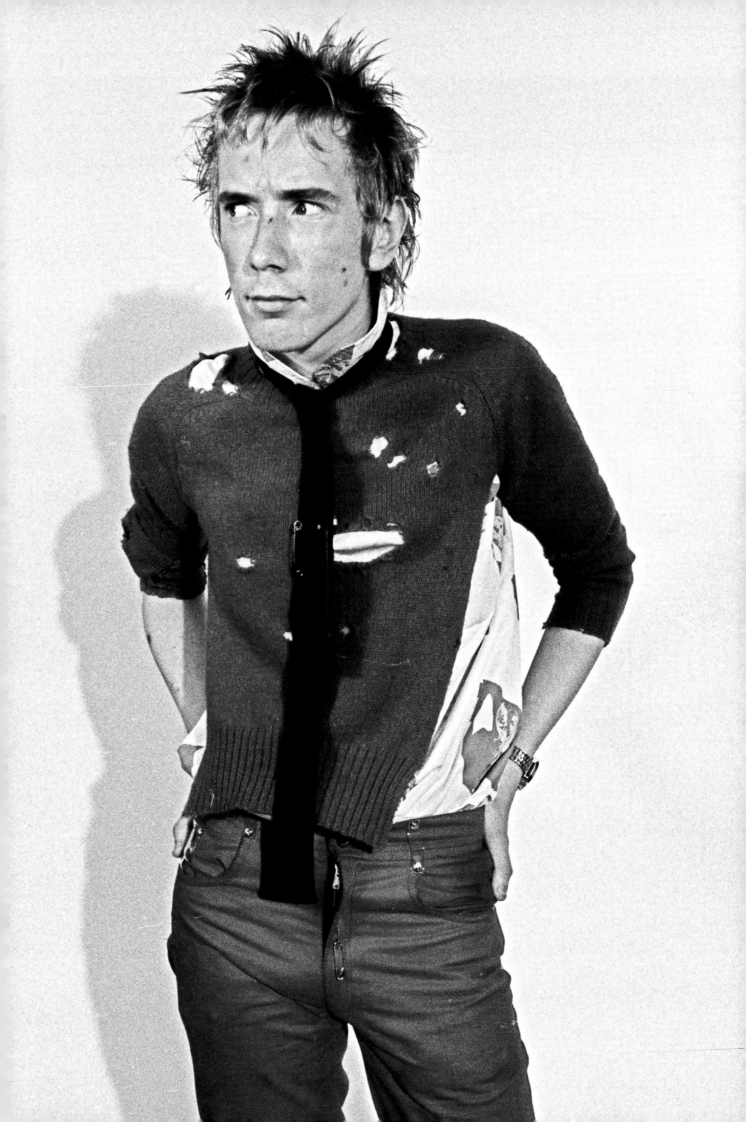

An extremely rare picture of John actually eating, late 1976. Authorities on the history of the Sex Pistols differ as to whether that is or is not Glen Matlock captured on the extreme left, making a fast grab for the olives and crisps...

Following pages: Woods Centre, Plymouth, 21 December 1976

Le Chalet de Lac, Paris, 3 September 1976

C FOR CHAOS

'All that talk about the French Revolution being associated with punk – what rubbish. Now that really is coffee-table punk.'

John Lydon, in Rotten: No Irish, No Blacks, No Dogs

Malcolm McLaren and John Lydon, March 1977. Not only are they not making eye-contact with each other, but the camera has caught them at a moment when the body language of both men does not seem to imply a total mutual complicity in the future of the Sex Pistols.

An introspective and somewhat serious John seems unaware that he is being photographed.
He also seems unaware that Jordan is playing up well by giving the photographer the two fingers.

"How many fingers am I holding up?"

O'Brien, in George Orwell's *Nineteen Eighty Four*

One thing that Lydon and McLaren genuinely shared was a loathing of seventies British television. The discovery of this shared dislike seems to date from their earliest encounters at the Roebuck in the King's Road, at the time when the Clash's to-be-manager Bernie Rhodes first persuaded Lydon to audition for the Pistols.

Looking back, you have to admit that they had a point. British television had lost whatever pioneering sprirt it might once have had. The last new channel to be launched had been BBC2, back in 1964. Instead of choice, an enforced consensus prevailed: a complacent worldview built around a rather smug and dated set of supposedly unifying British attitudes and preoccupations: sport, soaps, middlebrow comedy, middlebrow drama, middlebrow documentaries. This desperate and alienating state of affairs seemed at the time to be personified by ubiquitous middle-aged white male presenters such as Frank Bough - or Bill Grundy, if you like. Bough moved seamlessly from sport to news to eulogising bagpipe music without even changing his tweed jacket - and then found himself hounded into temporary obscurity by a press revelation of clandestine visits to an S&M dungeon in Chelsea.

McLaren and Rhodes had been influenced by the Situationist movement, and by the writings of its *defacto* leading spokesperson, Guy Debord. Debord's best-known work is *Society of the Spectacle* (*La Société du Spectacle*). In this work, and elsewhere, Debord argues that in advanced capitalist societies, the role of money as capital

and as a medium of exchange becomes subordinated to the role of the spectacle: what is seen, or what society chooses to regard as important, becomes its most significant measure of value. Arguably, McLaren's most crucial contribution to the Sex Pistols' legend was in assembling a group of individuals who could be relied upon to play the part expected of them as ambassadors of punk from the moment they were placed under the media spotlight. The media demanded spectacle, the Pistols required exposure: it was impossible for either to push the other too far.

The Pistols' round-the-houses malarkey with recording contracts - from EMI to A&M to Virgin - can be seen as being all part of the same media-savvy game. A band that usually performed live (when allowed to by local councils) in front of hundreds, rather than thousands, of fans, effectively captured the mainstream media agenda through a few well-timed outrages, such as the Grundy TV interview. By turning the moral panic of the media on the Sex Pistols, and using this energy to advertise the band to anybody out there who felt bored, discontented, or simply wanted to stick two fingers up at the establishment, McLaren pulled off one of the cleverest publicity stunts of all time. That is, if one sees McLaren as still being the Pistols' Svengali at this stage of their career.

But of course, moral outrage, like everything else, is finally subject to the law of diminishing returns...

Vivienne Westwood, Lydon and Jordan. Westwood's boiler-suit look, as seen here, would become mainstream high street fashion about three years later. By which time, Punk had morphed itself into New Wave (if the two movements were really connected), and the Sex Pistols had broken up.

GRUNDY: They are punk rockers. The new craze, they tell me. Their heroes? Not the nice, clean Rolling Stones... you see they are as drunk as I am... they are clean by comparison. They're a group called The Sex Pistols, and I am surrounded by all of them...

JONES: In action!

GRUNDY: Just let us see the Sex Pistols in action. Come on kids... [cut to film of the Sex Pistols in action] ... I am told that that group have received forty thousand pounds from a record company. Doesn't that seem, er, to be slightly opposed to their anti-materialistic view of life?

GLEN: No, the more the merrier.

GRUNDY: Really?

GLEN: Oh yeah.

GRUNDY: Well, tell me more then.

STEVE: We've fucking spent it, ain't we?

GRUNDY: I don't know. Have you?

GLEN: Yeah. It's all gone.

GRUNDY: Really? Good Lord?
Now I want to know one thing ...

GLEN: What?

GRUNDY: Are you serious or are you just making me... trying to make me laugh?

GLEN: No, it's gone. Gone.

GRUNDY: Really?

GLEN: Yeah.

GRUNDY: No, but I mean about what you're doing...

GLEN: Oh yeah.

GRUNDY: Are you serious?

GLEN: Mmm.

GRUNDY: Beethoven, Mozart, Bach and Brahms have all died ...

JOHN: They're all heroes of ours, ain't they?

Designer punk, 1976: a brand new twist. Johnny tries on the bondage gear for the first time, allegedly in Notting Hill.

GRUNDY: Really? What? What are you saying, sir?

JOHN: They're wonderful people.

GRUNDY: Are they?

JOHN: Oh yes! They really turn us on.

GRUNDY: Suppose they turn other people on?

JOHN: Well that's just their tough shit.

GRUNDY: It's what?

JOHN: Nothing. A rude word. Next question!

GRUNDY: No, no. What was the rude word?

JOHN: Shit.

GRUNDY: Was it really? God, you frighten me to death.

JOHN: Oh alright, Siegfried…

GRUNDY: What about you girls behind?

GLEN: He's like yer dad ain't he, this geezer. Or your Grandad.

GRUNDY: Are you worried or just enjoying yourself?

SIOUXSIE: Enjoying myself.

GRUNDY: Are you?

SIOUXSIE: Yeah.

GRUNDY: Ah! That's what I thought you were doing.

SIOUXSIE: I've always wanted to meet you.

GRUNDY: Did you really?

SIOUXSIE: Yeah.

GRUNDY: We'll meet afterwards, shall we?

STEVE: You dirty sod. You dirty old man.

GRUNDY: Well keep going, chief. Keep going. Go on, you've got another ten seconds. Say something outrageous.

STEVE: You dirty bastard.

GRUNDY: Go on, again.

STEVE: You dirty fucker!

GRUNDY: What a clever boy.

STEVE: You fucking rotter!

GRUNDY: Well that's it for tonight. I'll be seeing you soon. I hope I'll not be seeing you again. From me though, goodnight.

The Bill Grundy interview, 1 December 1976.

September 1976 Seditionaries publicity shots of the band, with
members of the Bromley Contingent and others added to ramp up the
punk credibility. Left to right: Nils Stevenson, Helen Wellington-Lloyd
(aka Helen of Troy), Paul Cook, Steve Jones, Debbie Wilson, Steve
Severin (later of Siouxsie and the Banshees) Siouxsie Sioux herself,
Glen Matlock, Johnny Rotten.

John in the Seditionaries gear.

Glen Matlock and Helen Wellington-Lloyd.

Steve Jones and Debbie Wilson.

Siouxsie Sioux , more or less wearing
the outfit that excited Bill Grundy's interest.

Another Seditionaries promo shot
from the same session.

Siouxsie and Paul

John and Siouxsie Sioux

Another group shot

WHY
THE UK

'Also da kann ich Fucker nur zustimmen..!!' 2005 post on a German punk website

'We shall do everything we can to restrain their public behaviour.' Sir John Read, EMI Chairman

For a band that were garnering so much media attenion, the Sex Pistols' schedule during late1976 and the early months of 1977 was not as busy as one might expect. With 'Anarchy In The UK' charting at number 38, the conventional music business management move would have been to get out there and play to the fans, promote the existing product and what was to come. But McLaren was forced to operate in a rather different way. With only a handful of towns and venues in the UK being prepared to allow the Pistols to play, the 'Anarchy' tour (also featuring The Damned, The Clash, and Johnny Thunders) telescoped into just three dates in December, one in Leeds and two in Manchester.

On 4 January, there was further trouble with the UK press, when the Pistols allegedly swore, vomited and spat in the departure lounge at Heathrow. The band were en route to Holland to appear on television and to play a couple of club gigs. This was the last straw as far as EMI's management were concerned, and on 6 January EMI withdrew from their recording contract with the band. EMI also curtailed production and marketing of 'Anarchy In The UK'. More trouble erupted in mid January, when Lydon was briefly arrested for possession of amphetamines. Everything came to a head in February, when Glen Matlock announced that he was leaving the band. (Other versions of the story claim that Matlock was fired, for reasons that range from 'liking the Beatles' to 'washing his feet all the time'.) Tabloid headlines had made the band into a household name of sorts, but the Sex Pistols now temporarily faced the future with no bass player and no record deal.

Meanwhile, across town, other British punk bands were beginning to make an impact on the public, the media and the music business. The first English punk band to have a hit single ('New Rose') were The Damned, a frantic four-piece fronted by former gravedigger Dave Vanian, usually dressed in a vampire costume. The Damned were signed in mid-1976 to Jake Riviera's label Stiff, and their debut album *Damned Damned Damned* was produced by the trans-generational Nick Lowe, whose CV included a spell with early seventies Country Rock contenders Brinsley Schwartz. *Damned Damned Damned*, released in February 1977, was the first British punk album in the shops. With its classic custard pie cover, and several memorable songs (including 'Neat Neat Neat'), it established The Damned as major contenders - a role they were, perhaps surprisingly, unable to maintain. The next significant album release was the first, eponymously-titled Clash album. This recording established itself as the soundtrack for the spring and early summer 1977, 'Janie Jones', 'Remote Control' , 'I'm So Bored With the U.S.A.' and the rest blasting out from bedsits, squats and student bedrooms all across the land. With other punk acts such as the Buzzcocks putting out landmark records, and bands such as The Stranglers reinventing themselves for the new punk audience, the Sex Pistols would need to make a big impact in the early months of 1977 in order to remain the clear leaders of the pack.

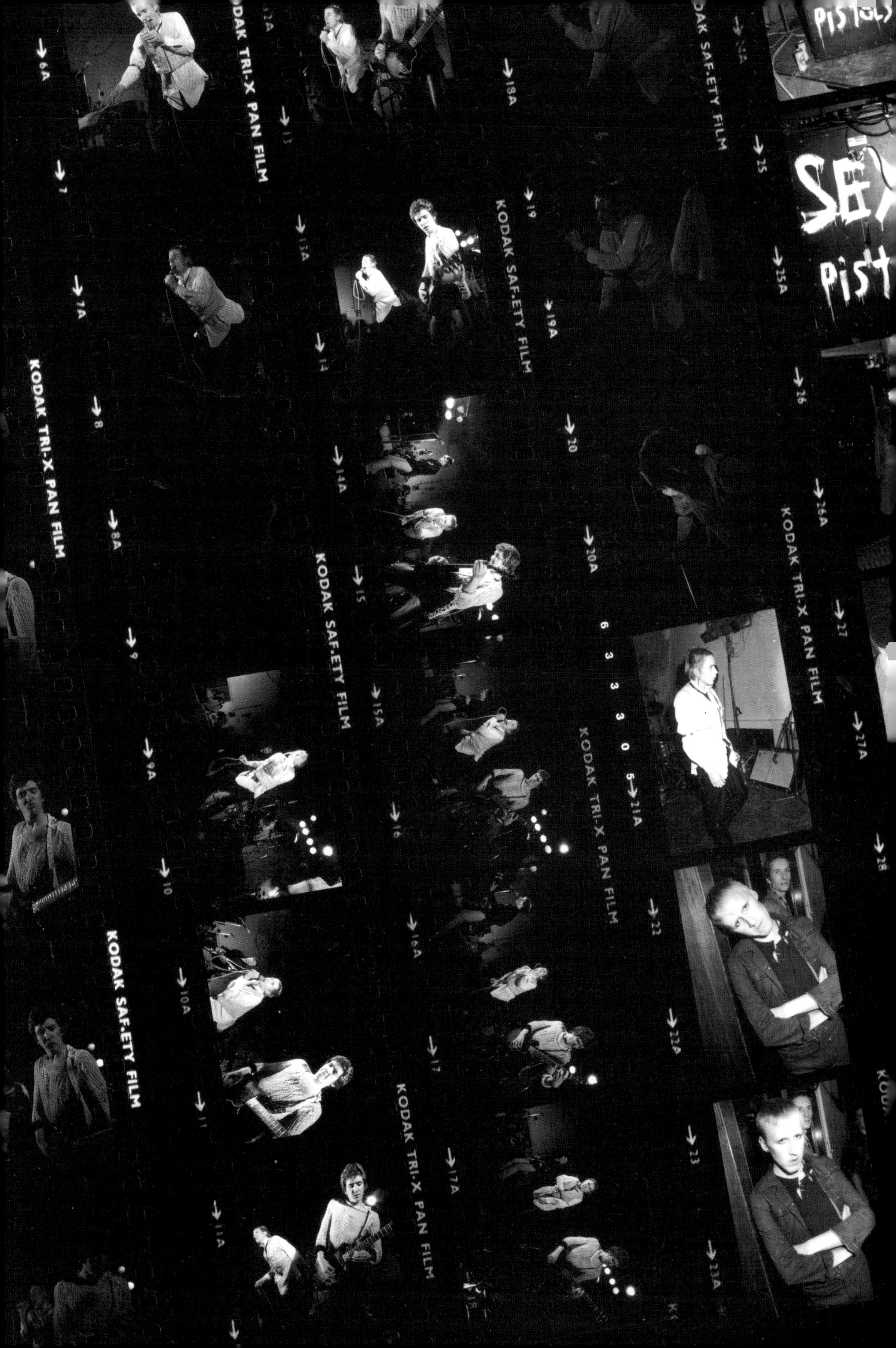
KODAK TRI-X PAN FILM
KODAK SAF.ETY FILM
6 3 3 0 5

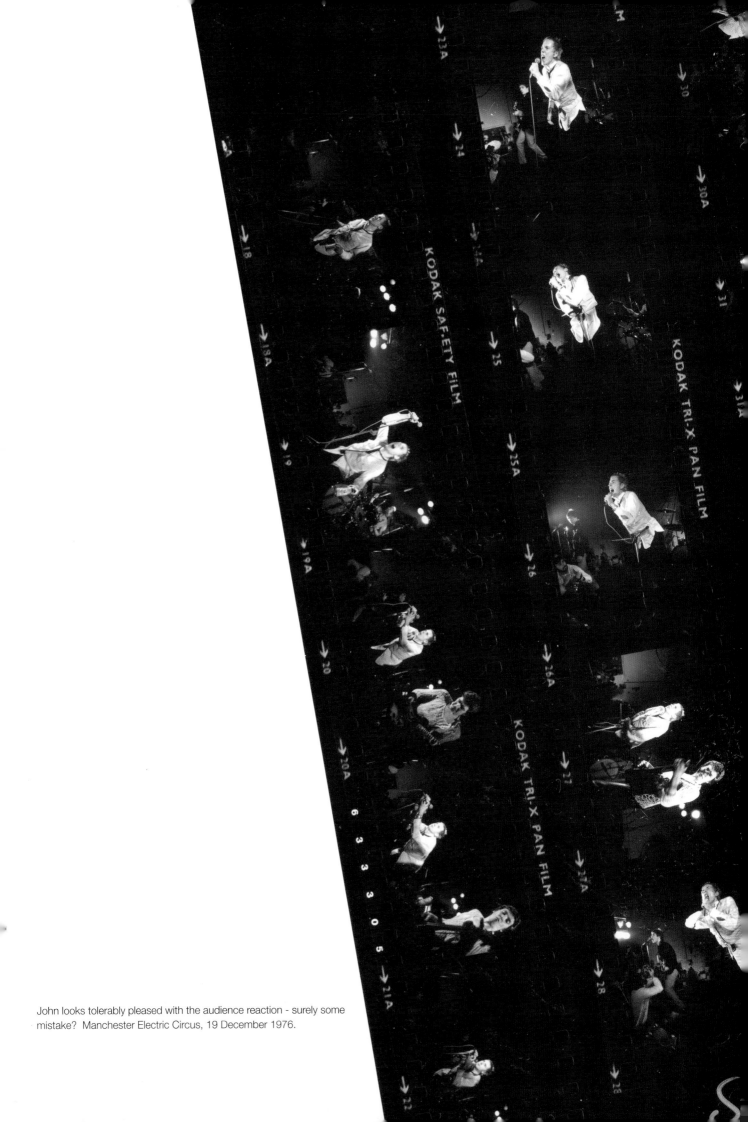

John looks tolerably pleased with the audience reaction - surely some
mistake? Manchester Electric Circus, 19 December 1976.

Woods Centre, Plymouth,
22 December 1976.

Steve Jones, Woods Centre, Plymouth,
22 December 1976.

KODAK TRI-X PAN FILM
KODAK SAFETY FILM
KODAK SAFETY FILM
KODAK TRI-X PAN FILM
12
12A
13
13A
14
14A
15
15A
16
16A

Friction between John and Glen Matlock became
increasingly apparent as 1976 drew to a close.

СИ АМ~Э УГОСЛ.ВИЛА

SUB STI

I want a fuck.
Eight inches of hard luck...

'Sid's the star' Nancy Spungen, 1978

John Ritchie (later to be known as Sid Vicious) was born in London on 10 May 1957. He was brought up by his mother, Anne Randal, but used his father's surname, although the two had never married. Anne later married Chris Beverly, who intended to adopt her son, but Beverly died before this was accomplished. Ritchie had an unstable and insecure childhood and adolesence, his mother being a heavy drug user with no regular source of income. Ritchie met John Lydon while both were attending Hackney & Stoke Newington College, and they roomed together afterwards in the same squat. After Lydon joined the Sex Pistols, Ritchie became the band's most loyal fan, and - on the occasion of Matlock's departure - he was invited to join the band. It has also been suggested that Lydon was keen to bring on board an old and trusted friend, to counterbalance the longstanding Cook-Jones axis within the band. McLaren reputedly saw in Ritchie's style and attitude his potential as a punk icon, perhaps more valuable to McLaren's schemes than any purely musical qualifications. John Ritchie became Sid Vicious, and was given Glen Matlock's role on bass, though compared to Matlock he was extremely inexperienced with the instrument. The

name Sid Vicious came from Lydon's pet hamster, a tiny furry creature that had been known to bite when provoked.

Meanwhile, McLaren had been holding meetings with Derek Green of A&M Records, with a view to securing the Pistols a new recording contract. A £30,000 settlement was also agreed with former label EMI over the annulled contract. On 13 February, a deal was agreed between McLaren and A&M, at a time when Glen Matlock was still (at least officially) the Pistols' bass player. But by the time the deal with A&M had been formalised, Matlock was gone and Sid Vicious had arrived as his replacement. Although by no means the whole story, this unexpected change of line-up may have contributed to the band's ultra-short stay at A&M. After signing with A&M on 8 March and staging a publicity-stunt re-signing on 9 March outside Buckingham Palace, A&M had second thoughts and fired the band one week later. Once again, the Pistols' and their management got to keep the £75,000 advance. Whatever may have been said subsequently, this profitable ruse was widely admired by many fans at the time. A&M also destroyed almost the entire pressing of 'God Save The Queen',

The staged contract signing outside Buckingham Palace.

but also gave the Pistols a £75,000 golden handshake. Lydon's view is that A&M, like EMI, got cold feet over the strong political content of the Pistols' music.

'It came as quite a shock, when the signing took place, that Glen Matlock wasn't in the band. It had been Matlock's name all the way through negotiations, and then on the day there was Sid Vicious, an unknown quantity.'

Derek Green, Managing Director, A&M Records

After the Buckingham Palace publicity stunt, all those concerned moved on to the A&M offices for a celebratory party, which is said to have turned into a bit of a drunken orgy. Historians of the band claim that Steve Jones entered the ladies toilet in search of female companionship, while Sid Vicious threw up all over the Managing Director's desk. Or maybe it was Lydon - accounts differ. Whatever the truth of these allegations, A&M terminated the Pistols' contract on 16 March.

On 12 May, it was announced that the Sex Pistols had signed to Richard Branson's label, Virgin. Lydon was suspicious of Branson's Public School hippy background, but Virgin had by 1977 grown into a major record label (chiefly on the strength of Mike Oldfield's recordings). A major label was what the Sex Pistols needed to give them presence in the marketplace. Low-key credibility on a small, independent record label was never part of the plan.

On 9 March 1977: the band, now compisring Johnny Rotten, Paul
Cook, Steve Jones and Sid Vicious, signed a new recording contract
with A&M. The next day, the signing was reprised outside Buckingham
Palace, for the benefit of television cameras. Malcolm McLaren and
a low-key Police presence made up the numbers. (The first A&M
Pistols' single was scheduled to be 'God Save the Queen' - geddit?).
Reputedly, Sid Vicious and Paul Cook had become involved in fight on
the way to the signing, after Vicious called Cook 'an albino gorilla'.

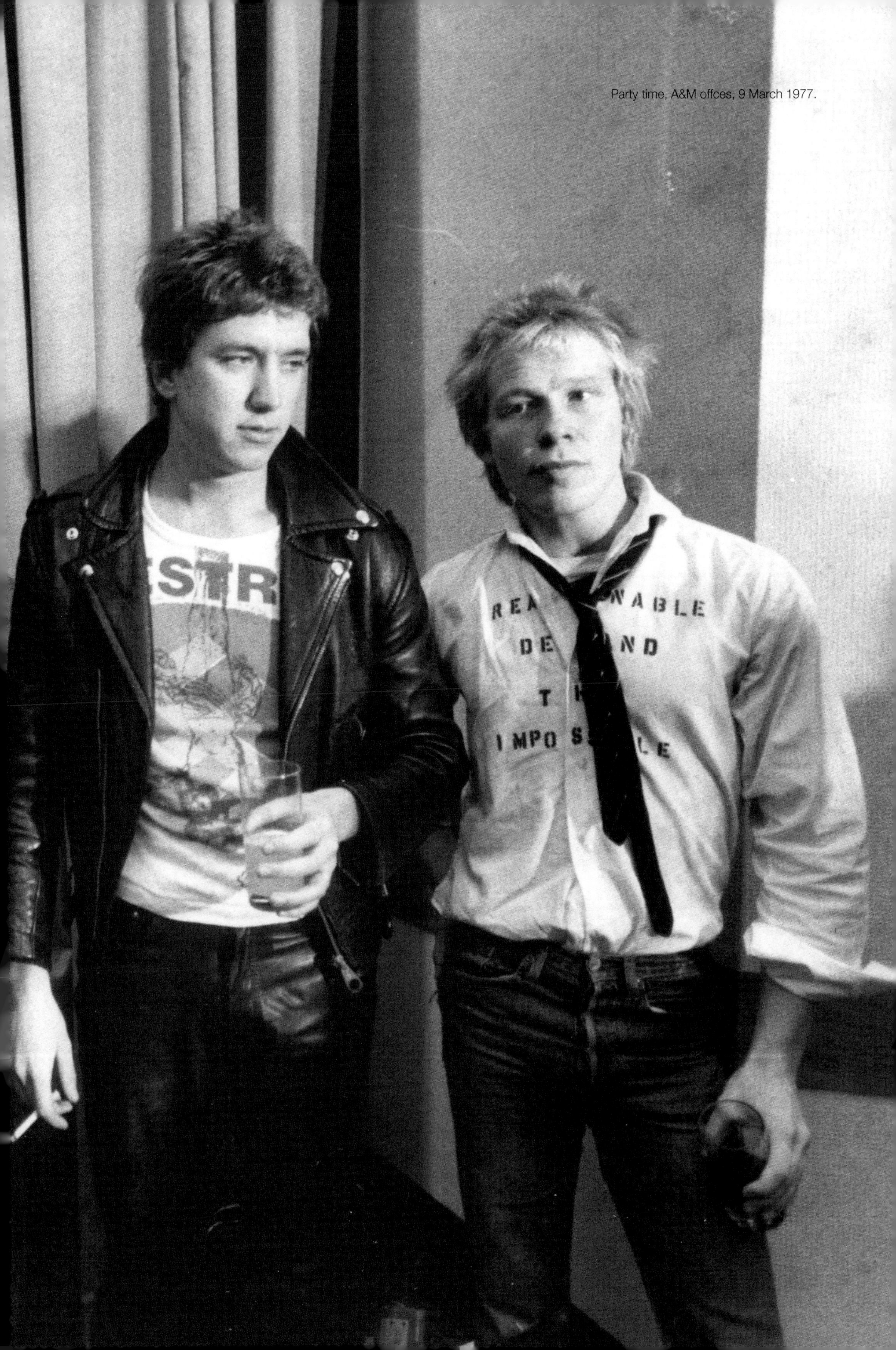

Party time, A&M offces, 9 March 1977.

A&M contract well and truly signed,
Sid gets down to some serious drinking

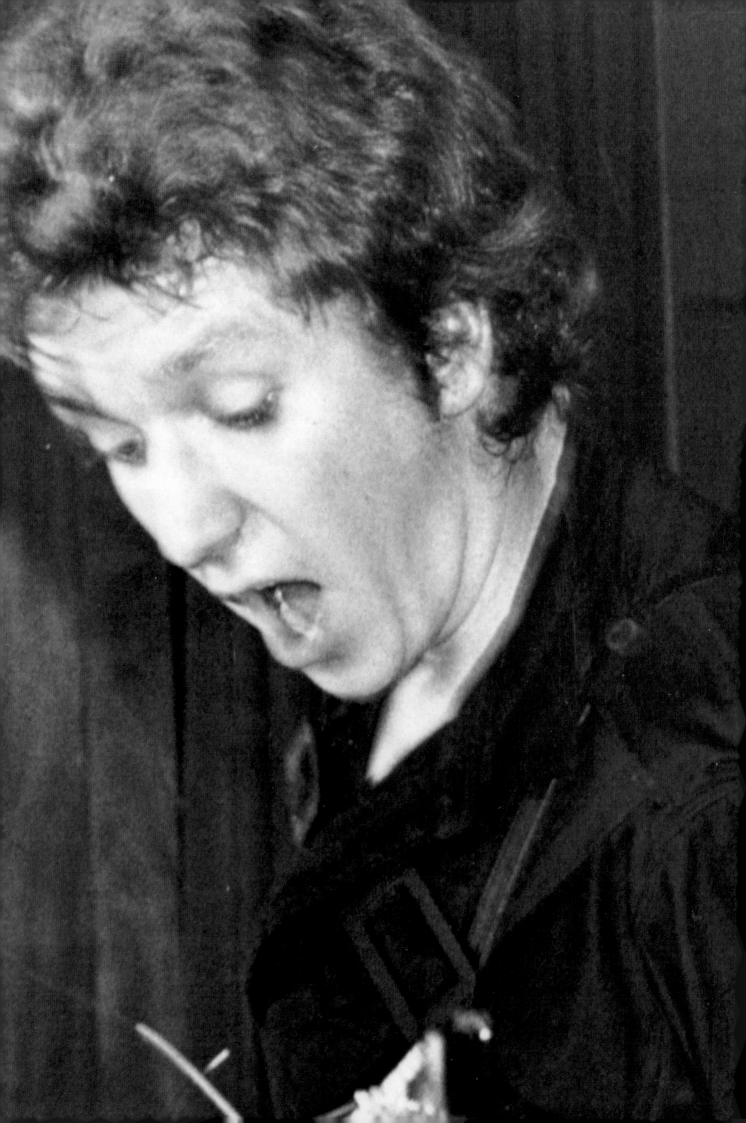

Notre Dame Hall, London, 21 March 1977. Filming for US NBC TV, Sid's first live appearance with the Sex Pistols.

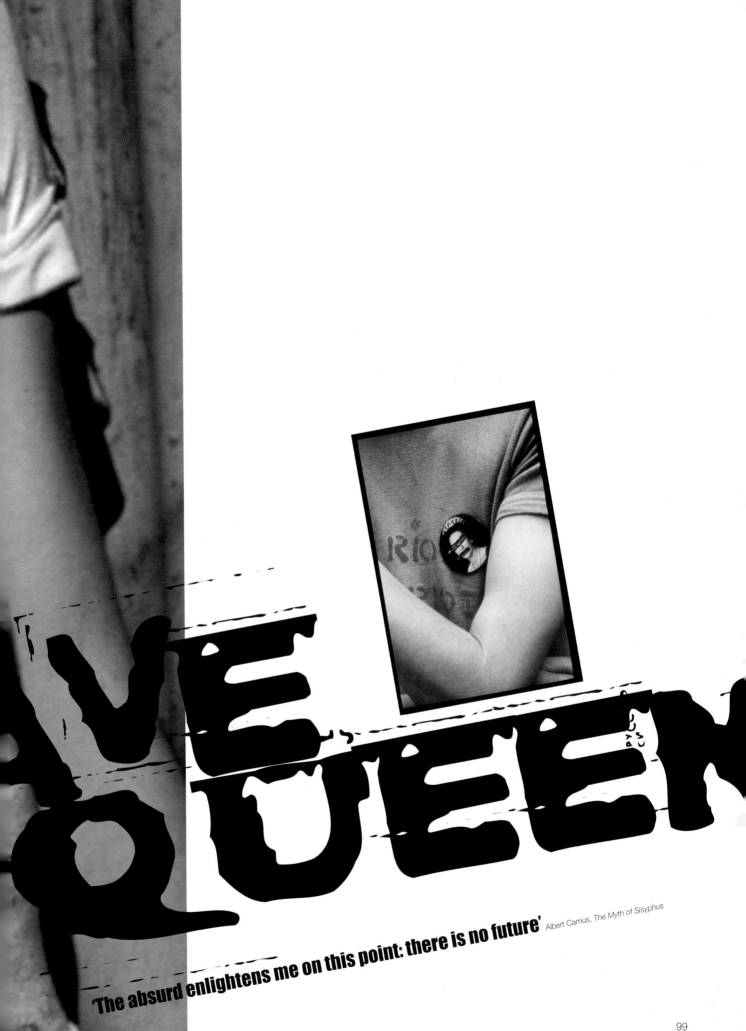

VE QUEEN

'The absurd enlightens me on this point: there is no future' Albert Camus, The Myth of Sisyphus

Jamie Reid's original banned cover artwork
for the single 'God Save the Queen'.

'...whining at the weather and the declining fortunes of the country, and wallowing nostalgically in gossip about the doings of the Royal Family and your so-called aristocracy in the pages of the most debased newspapers in the world. Tiger Tanaka of the Japanese Secret Service sums up the British malaise to James Bond in Ian Fleming's *You Only Live Twice*

In a spirit of impartiality and absolute fairness to all points of view, it has to be admitted that there are some people who claim that they had a very good time during the 1977 Royal Jubilee. The Queen and Prince Phillip led the Jubilee procession in the golden state coach, down the Mall, through Trafalgar Square, along Fleet Street and up Ludgate Hill to St Paul's Cathedral. Around the country, there were plenty of street parties, and plenty of good clean fun to be had by all, especially for those under seven or over 70 years of age. Nevertheless, you did not have to be a would-be Johnny Rotten to sense something a little tired and flyblown about Britain's attempt to puff itself up into a patriotic frenzy in celebration of 25 years of Elizabeth II's reign.

What exactly did the country think it was celebrating, beyond it's continued survival? To a confrontational performer such as Lydon, the spectacle of the country celebrating via its symbols of the past resembled an ostrich with its head firmly stuck in the sand: 'England's Dreaming'. And there is a kind of angry idealism buried deep in the lyrics of the Pistols' Jubilee party-pooper record, 'God Save the Queen' - stop dreaming, wake up, get real. No sentiment could have been more calculated to cause offence at such a time. The BBC, as everyone knows, banned 'God Save The Queen', and its position at Number Two in the singles charts during Jubilee Week was left as an eloquent blank (vacant!) space. Most radio stations declined to play the record, or to acknowledge its existence in any way.

On Jubilee day itself, 7 June, the Sex Pistols and Malcolm McLaren, now in cahoots with Virgin's Richard Branson, upped the ante still further by hiring a launch for a Jubilee cruise party on the River Thames. The Sex Pistols famously launched into 'Anarchy in the UK' as the boat chugged past the Houses of Parliament, attracting the immediate attention of the police. More police appeared as the boat docked, and an astonishing number of famous or soon-to-be famous people were briefly arrested for various breaches of the Queen's peace, including Malcolm McLaren, Vivienne Westwood, McLaren's assistant Sophie Richmond, and graphic designers Ben Kelly, Alex McDowell and Jamie Reid.

'Several times during the 1970s the main chart provided by the British Market Research Bureau came under scrutiny. There were claims that the chart was being fixed and altered to suit the whims and fancies of certain record companies and artists.'

Tony Jasper, *The 70s: A Book of Records*

The Jubilee parade.

Neighbourhoods flew the flag...

Some tasty Jubilee sausages.

'My masterpiece! It's like a splinter under the nail.' Henry Miller, *Black Spring*

'I was pretty pissed off when I first heard the Sex Pistols' 'Pretty Vacant'. Malcolm had stolen that whole attitude from 'Blank Generation'. But ideas are free property - I stole shit, too' Richard Hell

It's difficult to imagine the Sex Pistols following the traditional rock star career trajectory - early gigs, build a following, recording contract, hit albums, more tours to bigger and bigger audiences, platinum albums, stadium concerts, and so on - onwards and upwards *ad infinitum*. From the start, from the arrival of Lydon, and certainly from the introduction of Sid Vicious, there was something inevitable about the band's implosion and self-destruction. Maybe it's impossible for a tight-knit group to be the conduit for so much negative energy, and yet stay together for very long. But, in terms of a traditional rock CV, the Pistols did have one blockbuster of an album in them, twelve songs that more or less define what British punk was about, and indelibly inscribed the Pistols' worldview onto vinyl. Who needs a follow-up to an album of such momentous, era-defining power as *Never Mind The Bollocks, Here's The Sex Pistols*?

Most of the material on the album wasn't all that new. Several of the songs had been previously recorded at the legendary (i.e. much-bootlegged) 1976 recording sessions supervised by underground producer Dave Goodman. The tracks originally recorded with Goodman included 'Pretty Vacant', 'No Feelings', 'Submission' and 'Anarchy in the U.K.' - the core of the *Spunk* album (once a bootleg) that enjoys mythic status among Pistols fans. But the tracks on *Never Mind The Bollocks* were re-recorded with producers Bill Price and Chris Thomas (who share the credit for the album equally). The album tracks were built-up in layers around Steve Jones' adrenaline-fuelled guitar riffs, which Jones was able to ad-lib in perfect time ('he was the metronome', recollects Price). Underneath the guitar overdubs were mixed Cook's 'dustbins falling down the stairs' drum sound, and bass (there is still some coyness about who actually played this instrument, but Glen Matlock is said to have been hired for the album as a session musician). Over the top went Lydon's snarling, sneering vocals. Despite the low-tech, no-nonsense, back-to-basics ethos of punk, *Never Mind The Bollocks* is a complex and elaborate production. But the technique is placed at the service of the desired sound - energy that sounds as raw and violent as any live perfomance, captured through sophisticated production and played by a band who were serious about making a landmark recording.

Never Mind The Bollocks was released on 28 October, the title and the cover artwork creating another mini moral panic, with one manager being arrested for displaying the promo poster for the album in the window of the Virgin store in Nottingham. Robin Hood: Nil, Sheriff of Nottingham: One. But the album continued to sell impressively, though it could only be shelved under the counter.

'Just walk into the shop and say to the assistant: "Have you got Bollocks?"' Paul, 1977

The Pistols spent the remainder of 1977 in seeming inactivity, though the notoriety of their album kept their name very much in the public eye. They had played a few British gigs during the late summer under various aliases, to sidestep the bans placed on them by local councils.

A Sex Pistols' movie was in the planning stage, but slipped out of pre-production after finance was withdrawn. Sid Vicious became involved in a bloody fight in a hotel room with his American girlfriend Nancy Spungen, which resulted in the police being called. The band rounded out the year with their last ever UK gig, a benefit concert for striking firemen. This concert is affectionately remembered by those who were there as probably the last occasion on which the band cut through all the bullshit and just played. On 30 December, the Sex Pistols' US visas finally came through, after various delays occasioned by members of the band having criminal records.

The Pistols' 14-day tour of the USA followed a strange path, working its way in a serpentine slither that stayed well below the Mason-Dixon line, through hardcore Redneck country (Atlanta, Memphis, Baton Rouge, San Antonio, Dallas, Tulsa), before terminating in San Francisco for a gig at the Winterland on 14 January. Some have suggested that McLaren's itinerary was a final, perverse gesture of defiance to the East Coast Punk community. New York audiences might have accepted the band in a manner that would have generated none of the headline-grabbing controversy that the Bible-belt route guaranteed. Whatever the motivations behind this counter-intuitive approach to the Pistols' US tour, the final gig in San Francisco was the only concert to be played in front of an audience of any significant size - reportedly, five thousand. Lydon concluded the performance with the memorable exit line 'ever get the feeling you've been cheated?' Three days later, Lydon had left the band. Sid Vicious, whose behaviour had become ever more unpredictable during the tour, travelled to New York, to be reunited with Nancy Spungen. McLaren, Cook and Jones departed for South America and a recording session with Great Train Robber Ronnie Biggs. Lydon, stranded penniless for a time in New York, visited Jamaica in company with Richard Branson, to advise Virgin on the development of its roster of reggae artists. Lydon later returned to the UK, to begin work on his next venture, Public Image Ltd. There was some talk of Lydon rejoining the band, but Lydon was now set on a totally different path. The Sex Pistols, in terms of anything that resembled their original incarnation, were now history.

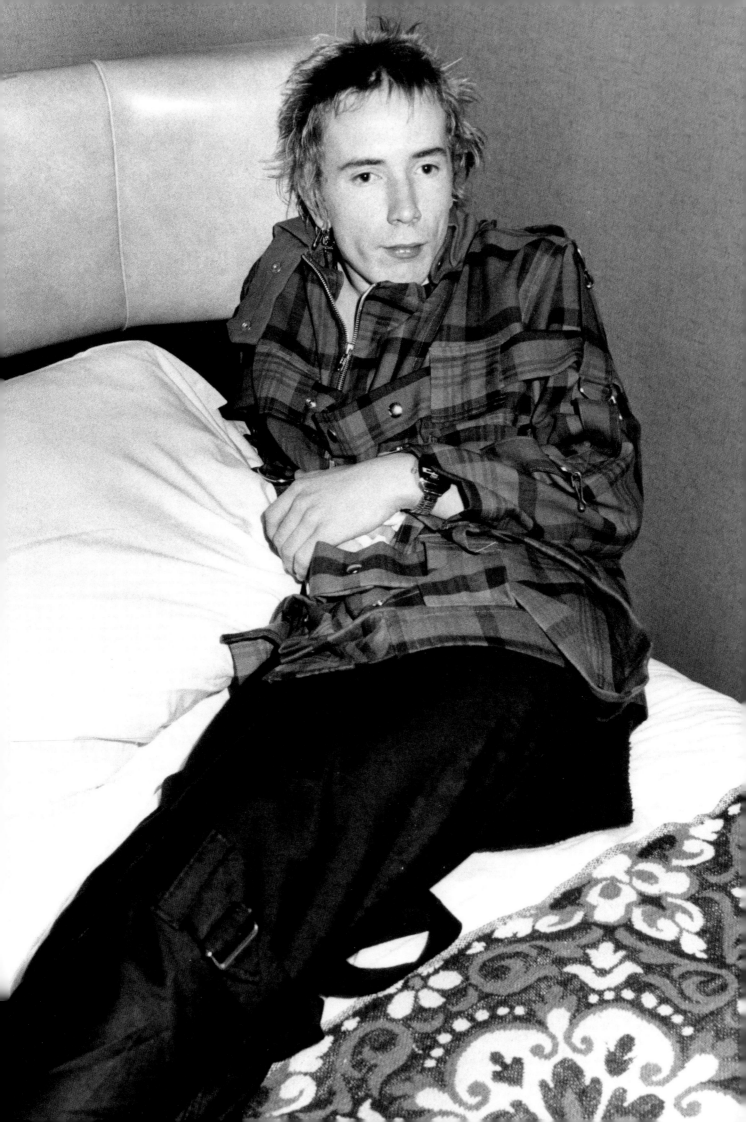

The Pistols (and McLaren) in the studio: some of Ray Stevenson's
brilliant portraits of the band at work.

116

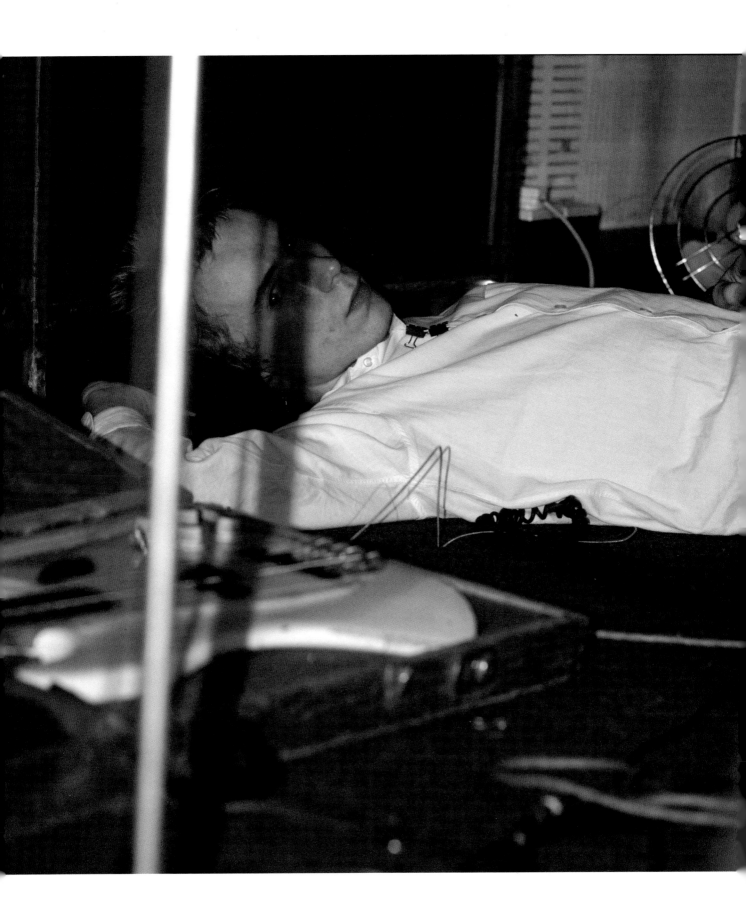

GRAND & TOY

LHR

It's all over. Lydon returns from Jamaica, March 1978.

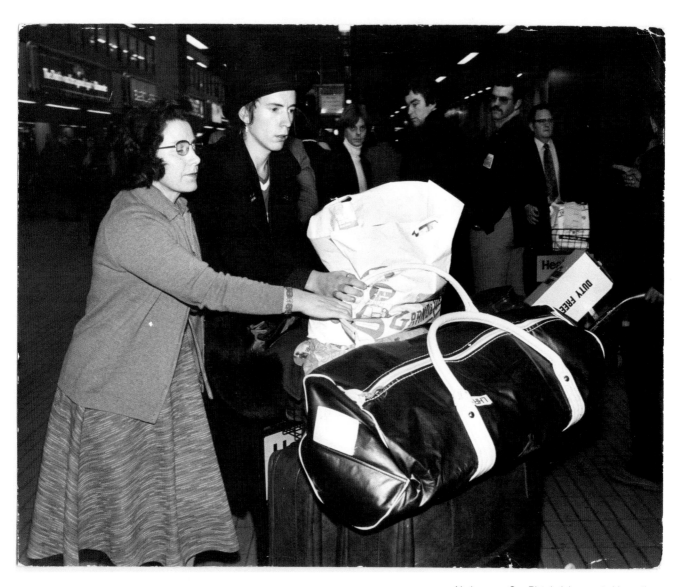

No longer a Sex Pistol, John meets his mother
on returning to London from the Jamaica trip.

'C'MON EVER

'It's not Punk, Henry, it's New Wave' Paul, 1977

'He is convinced that his film has somehow brought them into being'

Thomas Pynchon, *Gravity's Rainbow*

1978: the times they were a-changin'.

Of course, the Sex Pistols did not break up in January 1978. They continued in a kind of semi-existence for another two years, albeit transformed from a punk powerhouse to a kind of New Wave novelty act. There was the Ronnie Biggs single, the Sid Vicious 'My Way' cover, the album and film of *The Great Rock 'n' Roll Swindle*...

    The Great Rock 'n' Roll Swindle (1980) is what finally became of the long-awaited 'Sex Pistols movie'. Put together and edited after the band itself had effectively split up, it became the vehicle for Malcolm McLaren to relate a Situationist parable about the relationship between commerce and art, very loosely based on some of the incidents that had actually occurred. The story of the Sex Pistols was retold much later from a very different point of view and with different intent in *The Filth and the Fury* (2000). Both films are directed by Julien Temple, who is also responsible for such varied works as *Absolute Beginners* (1986), *Earth Girls Are Easy* (1988), *The Secret Policeman's Other Ball* (1982) and *At the Max* (1991)... aka *Rolling Stones: Live at the Max*. In *The Great Rock 'n' Roll Swindle,* McLaren presents himself as the genius and impresario who plotted and stage-managed the Sex Pistols' rise to stardom. Much praised at the time for its avant-garde editing and pastiche, 'mockumentary' technique, the movie does not even set out to tell the true story of the Pistols and as a result has, to say the least, become a bone of contention between McLaren and some members of the band. *The Filth and the Fury* (2000) sets out to redress the balance, but also provides through interpolated footage a penetrating portrait of the apathetic culture and political inertia that characterized mainstream British life in the mid-seventies. Unlike *The Great Rock 'n' Roll Swindle*, *The Filth and the Fury* provides a political and social context to the Pistols' career.

    As 1978 turned into 1979, records bearing the name Sex Pistols continued to be released. 'C'Mon Everybody', Sid Vicious's cover of the Eddie Cochrane classic, became the Pistols' second biggest UK hit, when it raced up to the number three position in the charts in August 1979. An ironic end, if there ever was one. Ever get the feeling you've been cheated?

The Great Rock 'n' Roll Swindle finally comes to town.

This is the absolutely pukka photograph of Steve Jones with Olivia Newton-John. Both stars celebrate September birthdays (3 and 26 respectively), though they are not the same star sign: Steve being a Virgo, while Olivia is a Libra.

Jordan in Cannes, May 1978

mas·cu·line /'mas-kye-len/ adj
[ME masculin, fr. MF, fr. L mas-
culinus, fr. masculus, n., male,
dim. of mas male] 1 a : MALE b :
2 : of, relating to, or con-
stituting the gender that ordi-
includes most words or
matical forms referring to
3 a : having or occurring in
ssed final syllable b : having
nal chord occurring on a
beat 4 : of or forming the
mas·cu·line·ly adv —mas·
/-len-nes/ n —mas·
,mas-kye-'lin-et-e/ n

Sid performing with the Vicious White Kids, Electric Ballroom, London, 15 August 1978. Left to right: Glen Matlock, Rat Scabies, Sid Vicious, Steve New.

FLOGGIN OEAO

'When cynicism sets in, I head for the hills' John Peel

'It is not the intensity but the duration of pain that breaks the will to resist' William Burroughs, The Naked Lunch

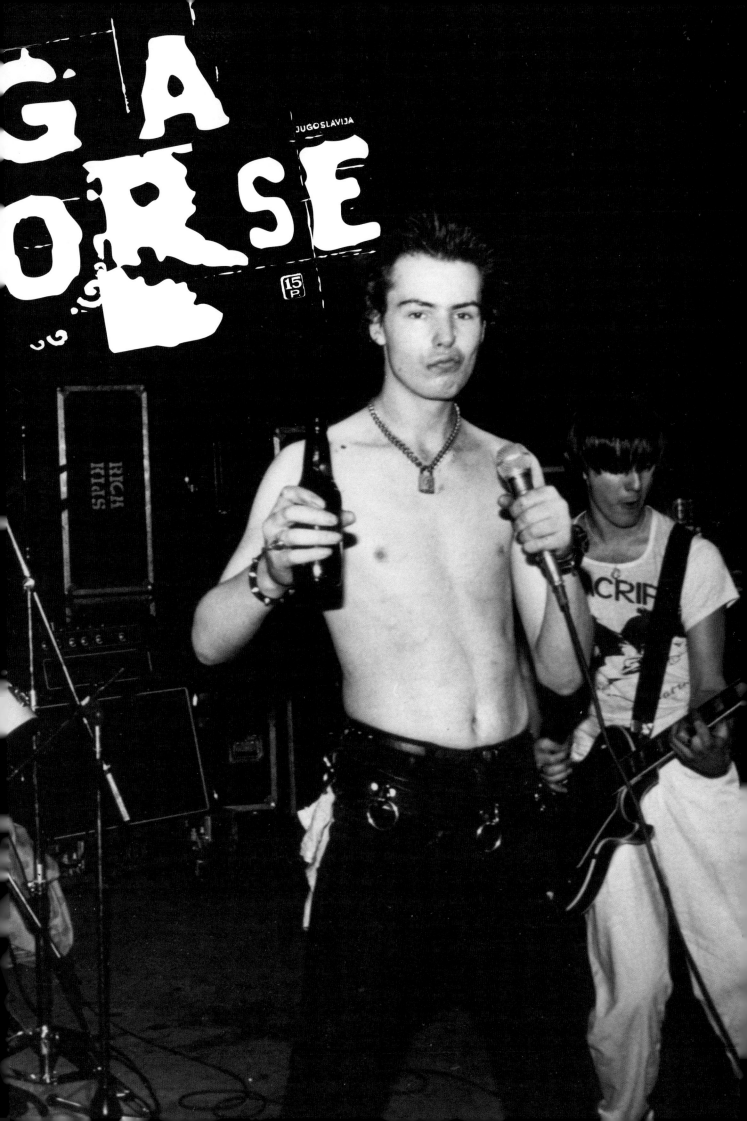

ENNE WESTWOOD

Vivienne Isabel Swire was born on 8 April 1941, in Derbyshire, England. After studying at a teacher training college, she taught in a primary school in North London in the 1960s. After the breakup of her first marriage to Derek Westwood, she became involved with Malcolm McLaren. In 1972 they co-launched the Chelsea boutique Let It Rock. After the huge impact of the Sex Pistols and punk fashion, Westwood and McLaren became a major force in the New Romantic fashion movement, with the swashbuckling Pirate collection. Westwood separated from McLaren and relocated to Italy in 1983, producing the Witches (1983) and Clint Eastwood (1984) collections. The bold and irreverant use of historical themes for contemporary collections became something of a Westwood trademark, with Dangerous Liaisons, Pagans and Anglomania being other themed collections. Westwood's fashion label has grown into a worldwide success. In 2004-5 she was honoured by a retrospective of her work at the Victoria and Albert Museum, London, and the National Gallery of Australia.

Admired by many, but not all. Lydon
recently compared Vivienne Westwood
to Margaret Thatcher.

MALCOLM McLAR

Malcolm McLaren was born in London on 22 January 1946. He attended several art colleges after school, including Saint Martins, Harrow and Goldsmiths. During this eight-year stretch as a student, he developed his interest in fashion design. In 1972 he teamed up with partner Vivienne Westwood to open a boutique in the King's Road, and also worked as a costume designer for the film industry, including work on *Mahler* for maverick director Ken Russell. McLaren gained his first experience of band management in 1974, taking over the career of proto-punk band The New York Dolls, before retuning to London and the Chelsea boutique in 1975.

After completing *The Great Rock 'n' Roll Swindle*, Malcolm McLaren was in need of new worlds to conquer. He briefly took over management of the then-struggling Adam and the Ants, who became transformed from second-division punks into avatars of the junior end of the New Romantic movement, with a string of hit singles and two monster albums. McLaren also took over Adam's previous Ants, teamed them up with teenage singer Annabella Lwin, and guided the resulting band, Bow Bow Wow, through a brief but controversial career. In 1983, television pundits began pronouncing on 'Malcolm McLaren's latest discovery: himself' as McLaren launched his own career as frontman with the rap-influenced 'Buffalo Girls', followed up by 'Double Dutch'. In 1985, McLaren recorded a version of 'Madame Butterfly' that entered the British charts. Subsequent non-music projects took McLaren away from music and to Hollywood, although various re-mixes and outtakes of earlier recordings have surfaced from time to time. Other music-related projects McLaren has been involved in included the launch of girl-band Jungk in 1998, and a conversion to Bitpop electronic music in 2003. McLaren has also been suggested as a possible candidate to stand against Ken Livingstone as the Mayor of London.

Mugshot taken by the NYPD after Sid Vicious's arrest in October 1978 for the murder of Nancy Spungen.

A different style: Steve Jones in 1987.

After the Sex Pistols' demise, Paul Cook formed The Professionals with Steve Jones: the first Professionals album *I Didn't See It Coming* was delayed for some time, but emerged at the end of 1981, containing the band's signature track 'Kick Down The Doors'. Cook later joined the much-praised but ultimately unsuccessful Chiefs of Relief in 1985, with former Adam and the Ants guitarist Matthew Ashman. In the 1990s Cook also worked with ex-Orange Juice frontman Edwyn Collins. Aside from ongoing Sex Pistols tours, Paul is also the drummer in Man-Raze.

After the Professionals broke up, Steve Jones played with Thin Lizzy, Joan Jett and others, as well as pursuing a solo career, relocating to Los Angeles. Jones was also a key component of the Sex Pistols tours of 1996 and 2002-3. In 2004 he began hosting a daily radio show in Southern California known as 'Jonsey's Jukebox',

playing a highly personal and eclectic mix of music.

Sid Vicious remained officially a Sex Pistol until the end. On the morning of 12 October 1978, Sid awoke in New York's Hotel Chelsea to discover Nancy Spungen dead in the bathroom, the apparent cause of death being a stab wound. Vicious was arrested and charged with Spungen's murder, although he was bailed at the expense of Virgin Records and with the support of McLaren. During his stay in Rikers Island prison Vicious apparently underwent rehabilitation for his heroin addiction. But shortly after his release on bail in February 1979, he was found dead, having overdosed. The solo album *Sid Sings* was released by Virgin later in 1979, including the singles 'My Way' and 'C'mon Everybody'. He also, of course, made a posthumous appearance in *The Great Rock 'n' Roll Swindle*.

On leaving the Sex Pistols in January 1978, Johnny Rotten once more became John Lydon, and set about forming a new band, Public Image Ltd. PiL's initial line-up also included Lydon's old friend Jah Wobble on bass, ex-Clash guitarist Keith Levene, and young Canadian drummer Jim Walker. PiL's first album was the well-received *First Issue*, with Wobble's deep bass and Levene's guitar making an incisive contribution, and Lydon's vocals sounding more penetrating than when with the Pistols. *Metal Box* followed in 1979, recorded with various drummers and achieving a spare, spacy sound influenced by both reggae and *avant garde* German band Can. The album kept PiL at the forefront of the post-New Wave British *avant garde*, and was heavily played by cult radio DJ John Peel. However, things became more stormy in 1980, with some under-rehearsed PiL gigs, a constant turnover of drummers, and some splendidly chaotic television appearances. Wobble departed, and PiL recorded *Flowers of Romance,* an even more inaccessible recording than *Metal Box.* In 1982 there was a live album, *Live in Tokyo*, and then a more commerical release in 1985, *This Is What You Want, This Is What You Get.* 'When cynicism sets in, I head for the hills' commented Peel on this record's release. More albums from PiL followed at irregular intervals, until Lydon formally disbanded the project in 1993, with ex-Smiths' drummer Mike Joyce being the final occupant of the PiL drum stool. Cream rhythm section Jack Bruce and Ginger Baker also put in a stint in PiL. Lydon's major post-PiL music venture was the 1997 solo album, *Psycho's Path*.

John at home in Gunter Grove, Autumn 1978.

PUBLIC IMAGE LTD

THE METAL
PUBLI

ONY®
ROOUB

London Press Conference, 16 May 2002.

Left: John and wife Nora
Right: Q Music Awards, Park Lane Hotel, 2001.

THE SWINDLE CONTINUES..

'This teenage thing is getting out of hand' Colin MacInnes, Absolute Beginners

"What are you going to be doing ten years from now?" I asked a visiting radical in the house where Spider is put together. "What if there's no revolution by then, and no prospects of one?" "Hell" he said. "I don't think about that. Too much is happening right now. If the revolution's coming, it had better come damn quick." Hunter S Thompson, *The Great Shark Hunt*

In 1996, the original Pistols line-up of Rotten, Cook, Jones and Matlock was reunited for a series a UK dates, dubbed the Filthy Lucre tour.

Kicking off in Finsbury Park (Lydon's birth-place) on 23 June 1996, the tour was timed to coincide with the twentieth anniversary of the long, hot summer of 1976. The band's set-list consisted of all the classics from *Never Mind The Bollocks:* 'Pretty Vacant', 'EMI', 'Anarchy in the UK' 'No Fun', 'Problems'. This might have seemed to some cynics like the kind of golden oldies show aimed at middle-aged fans that Bob Dylan, The Rolling Stones, Paul McCartney and others had been purveying for many years, but the tour was justified by Steve Jones on the grounds that the original Pistols' incarnation had only ever played about 50 gigs. So the songs, although 20 years old, were hardly over-exposed in live performance.

A further reunion concert was organized at the Crystal Palace bowl in 2002 - the Sex Pistols' own Jubilee, as Lydon was happy to point out. This gig was followed the next year by a brief North American tour - only the second the band had ever undertaken. Not all the personal recriminations between the Pistols had necessarily been healed, but Lydon in particular seemed to enjoy himself on these tours. The band, he said, had learned how to unite in the face of the rest of the world. Asked in 2002 if he had a message for the fans, he answered 'Don't think I'm any better than you, I'm probably a lot worse.... If you've got something you do and it's better than the way I do what I do, then question me. But until you've actually made a commitment to the human race, shut the fuck up.'

In early 2004, the British media were presented with a gift of a 'celeb' gossip story: John Lydon was set to participate in the new series of *I'm A Celebrity... Get Me Out Of Here!* Not that all of the media were impressed by this news. Former *New Musical Express* scribe Charles Shaar Murray was moved to comment in *The Guardian* '"Whatever happened to punk rock, maaaaan?' Lydon's loyal fans were more positive about their man's

participation in this celebrity equivalent of *Big Brother*, the consensus being that the show represented an opportunity for John to convert a whole new generation of fans.

In the event, the fans were right. Lydon effortlessly upstaged the other contestants, famously picking a fight with princessy glamour model Jordan (no relation to the seventies punk icon). After taking an early lead in viewer popularity polls, he suddenly quit in a bout of swearing, gaining more publicity than the winner and yet managing to distance himself from the show's ideology of inane celebrity worship. A masterful performance. Even an ITV spokeswoman was moved to describe John as 'an endearing, eccentric and sensitive character.'

The re-formed Pistols hit London. Looking just a little bit older, but full of vim and vigour, Cook, Lydon, Jones and Matlock explore the West End together in March 1996, at the start of their UK Filthy Lucre Tour tour.

Paris, Le Zenith, 4 July 1996.

A genial looking Glen Matlock, 1995.

PUNK
FILTH...

By Garth Pearce and Patrick C...

CONCERTS for the Sex Pi... were cancelled and intervi... Bill Grundy was suspended ... in a row over the gr... outburst on TV. ...real four-letter ... CASH. For ...

BRITAIN'S Thursday ...

February 2004: John flies to Australia to appear in the reality show *I'm a Celebrity, Get Me Out of Here*. The ex-Pistol's fellow contestants included ex-BBC royal correspondent Jennie Bond, ex-DJ Mike Read, ex-footballer George Best's estranged wife Alex, ex-pop star Peter Andre, ex-athlete Diane Modahl, ex-insurance fraudster Lord Brocket, ex-footballer Neil Ruddock, ex-Atomic Kitten Kerry McFadden, and Jordan, still pursuing her career as an unfeasibly big-breasted model. Jordan and Johnny, famously, didn't hit it off, and Lydon soon walked off the show.

'When the Sex Pistols let loose a few expletives on Bill Grundy's show back in 1976, there was all sorts of huffing and puffing. The nation went into what is referred to as a 'moral panic'…. When, last week, former Pistol frontman John Lydon uttered the word 'cunt' on I'm a Celebrity Get Me Out of Here, the reaction was decidedly pianissimo. Out of an audience of 12 million for the show, Lydon's c-word outburst solicited merely 88 complaints.' Patrick West, *sp!ked*

ACKNOWLEDGEMENTS

'Glory, as anyone knows, is bitter stuff'

Yukio Mishima, *The Sailor Who Fell From Grace With The Sea*

The spectacle is the developed modern complement of money where the totality of the commodity world appears as a whole, as a general equivalence for what the entire society can be and can do. The spectacle is the money which one *only looks at*, because in the spectacle the totality of use is already exchanged for the totality of abstract representation. The spectacle is not only the servant of *pseudo-use*, it is already in itself the pseudo-use of life.

Guy Debord, *Society of the Spectacle*

Thanks to: Adrian, Diane, Ed, Guy, Paul, Stef, Steve and all the *Scumbag* team, Kasper De Graaf, Malcolm Garrett, Andy Godfrey, Marcus Hearn, Glen Marks and everyone at Rex Features, Catherine McDermott and especially David Pratt, for tracking down the unseen images.

Special thanks: Phil Singleton, for help with dates and locations of many of the unpublished photographs.

Photographer Credits (all references are by page numbers)

David Allocca 144

David Batchelor 23

Marillo Carlos 153

David Dagley 30, 31

Everett Collection 96-97

Geoff Garratt 108

Fraser Gray 124-125

Dave Hogan 136-137

Nils Jorgensen 100, 130,132,133

Frank Monaco 104-105

Erik Pendzich 146

Jonathan Player 101

Kip Rano 103

Brian Rasic 142,143,151, back cover

Sheila Rock 11, 103, 128-129, 141

Nick Rogers 109

JF Roussier 152

Ray Stevenson 2, 7, 8-9, 10, 12-13, 14, 15, 16-17, 18-19, 20, 21, 22, 24, 25, 26, 27, 28-9, 41, 42, 43, 44, 52-53, 56-57, 58, 70-71, 92-93,116-121, front cover

Paul Revere 106, 107

John Selby 101

STI Photographs 138

Richard Young 33, 34, 35, 36, 37, 38, 39, 46, 54-55, 60-69, 74, 77, 81, 82-83, 84-85, 86-87, 88-89, 90-91,113,123,126,141,144,145,147,149

Sergio Zalis 99, 111

Further Reading:
DeBord, Guy, *Society of the Spectacle* (English language translation), Rebel Press, 1992
Hebdige, Dick, *Subculture: The Meaning of Style*, Routledge, 1979
Jasper, Tony, *The 70's: A Book Of Records*, Macdonald Futura, 1980
Lydon, John, Rotten: *No Irish, No Blacks, No Dogs*, Plexus, 2004
Matlock, Glen, Silverston, Pete, *I Was a Teenage Sex Pistol*, Omnibus, 1991
Monk, Noel E, *12 Days on the Road: The Sex Pistols and America*, William Morrow, 1992
Reynolds, Simon, *Rip It Up and Start Again: Postpunk, 1978–1984*, Faber, 2005
Savage, Jon, *England's Dreaming*, Faber, 2005
Walsh, Gavin, *God Save the Sex Pistols: A Collector's Guide to the Priests of Punk*, Plexus, 2003